THE AROMA
OF LILAC

ALSO BY SR INCIARDI

Coloring Outside the Edges
October 2022

The Aroma of Thawing, Poems on Grief and Recovery
May 2023

THE AROMA OF LILAC

Poems on Grief, Hope and Healing After Loss

SR INCIARDI

Copyright © 2025 SR Inciardi

All rights reserved. No part of this book may be reproduced or used in any manner without the prior written permission of the copyright owner, except for the use of brief quotations in a book review.

Hardcover ISBN: 979-8-9881543-6-5
Paperback ISBN: 979-8-9881543-7-2
eBook ISBN: 979-8-9881543-8-9

First Edition 2024; Second Edition 2025
Cover & Interior Design by Liliana Guia
Cover Illustration by ch123/Shutterstock.com

For Adelina, Liliana, Taylor, and Ryan

SECTION ONE

At the End of the World	12
Black Letters	14
Resistance	16
Hopes and Dreams	17
3:24	18
If Only	19
Chapters	20
The Aroma of Despair	21
Appearances	22
Another Day	23
Night Falling	24
Water Flowing	25
In Its Own Time	26
Grief's Whispers	28
Sunset's Fashion	29
Knowing	30
Marionette	31
As Well	32
Regret	33
Miserable Comfort	34
The Cloak	35
Broken Branches	36
Breaths	37
Soulful	38
Circuition	39
Callings	40
Unrequited	41
Phases	42
Pinky Swear	43
The Aroma of Disappointment	44
Grief	45
Days of Summer	46
Balance	47

SECTION TWO

Dispersion	50
Birth Dance	51
Postmortem	52
New Light	53
Sunlight in Fall	54
Vibes	55
Feel the Noise	56
Solstice Shadows	57
Early Morning Light	59
Occhi e Orecchie	60
Voices After Tragedy	62
A Pact With Nature	63
No Rest with Just Silence	65
The Moment At Evening	66
Hills	67
Sight for Sore Eyes	68
River in Autumn	69
Recollections of Water	70
Contentment Quotient	71
Beyond Question	72
Amber Sunrise	74
Rain Whispers	75
The Aroma of Hope	76
The Aroma of Lilac	77
About the Author	78
Acknowledgments	79
Postscript	80

Poetry by SR Inciardi

The Aroma of Lilac, Poems on Grief, Hope and Healing After Loss is a collection of poems on grieving and attempting to live with the loss of a loved one. The collection explores the vulnerabilities of being human, trying to understand our place on earth, celebrating happiness (when possible), facing our own death and the curiosities of an afterlife, acknowledging regrets and the limitations of being human—all while trying to be resilient.

In 2022, the author's son passed away after a short bout with Influenza. He left behind a wife, two young daughters, his parents, a sister and brother-in-law, and many friends and work associates. His passing was a shock to everyone. Outside of the productive and wonderful aspects of his short time on earth, it seemed that little good came from his untimely passing. This book and another the author released earlier entitled ***The Aroma of Thawing, Poems on Grief and Recovery*** do not replace what is missing but offer the one thing they can--hope to those in similar circumstances.

This is SR Inciardi's third collection of poetry.

Enjoy them.

SECTION ONE

At the End of the World

There came a time when earth settled,
when randomness was set aside
and what had come to be
is what since then has been,
perhaps a choice it made or was told to take
when trees swayed and birds sang aloud,
when squirrels searched and deer nuzzled the petite grasses,
in a time when rocks and rivers
coalesced, when jagged edges and white-water
were smoothed into visible routine, when what was expected
is what happened, century upon century.

But there comes a time when sunlight
becomes indistinguishable from night,
when the day is filled with thick clouds and somber music
and the earth is confused by what is cast upon it,
when everything that could be said was and nothing
changes the song now playing—a troubled season
when deer disappear and birdsong is emptied
and the rivers running have lost direction,
when rocks teeter then tumble
and nothing commands their end, this despair,
this end of the world.

This is the way the world then tastes,
the day melted into harshly-burnt chocolate
thickened to a disagreeable consistency,
when the end of an already somber day is at hand
and night overtakes what remains,
standing alone in the rush of darkness
engulfing everything.

Yet rivers flow and rocks still stand
through the dark night,
through silence and stillness,
changed but present, each one in a place
with which I'm familiar. When the end
is just the start of what is thrust upon it
and any sketch of what had been drawn
is redrafted, the old forcibly set aside,
the same dawn coming to a world
now completely different.

Black Letters

For my son, Rick

The paper says you died
    and notes, in black letters,
        the demon that put you down.

How can simple black letters
    simplify the majesty of the sun
        or the glimmer of stars in a calm night sky?

How do a few words capture the elegance of sunset
    or the glory of early morning? How does rushing rain,
        gathering what has fallen,

not take it in its caress,
    its cleansed breath whispers the words
        that replace older ones.

What is the truth of this world,
    is it the black letters or the patter of steady rain
        in night's darkness, the red streaks

of an evening sky against the blue-cast mountains,
    or the journey of the black saw-wing in spring?
        All will come no matter what,

unaltered they will soar above the black letters
gathered on paper, and those who left
will know the will of sunrise and cheer

even if they can no longer offer words or a touch,
they will travel through each moment
with their own eyes to still witness.

Resistance

I resist.
I do not consent.
    I still expect to be made whole.
I demand restitution:
    for words that can no longer be spoken,
    for moments that can only be recalled.

This is justice's deafness.
I demand the universe relent, hear me,
acknowledge what I've lost!
    Soothe my anger!
    Apologize!

I will no longer know inner peace
the sun will no longer greet me
    quite the same way:
each morning its soft hands
    will no longer prod me awake,
the beautiful earth scarred, the sounds of its music
    of a cadence I do not know
    cannot follow.

Hopes and Dreams

What is your purpose?
What is it you want?

Is it worship?   Praise?
I see what rotates in blue and white
and through the blackness circling like a shark
where calamity can strike in a moment.

Why is this the dogma of your trialing,
the stark will, the parables we're told
to lean into each day, and in a world
so deceptively beautiful. Yet it's hard
to keep going each day, the demands you impose
whether we ourselves tempt fate
or are bewildered by your challenges,
under belief or in the ignorance of bluster
trying to stay positive when so much is at the edge
of jeopardy. But adversity assures you change
me into something I hadn't planned, unable to turn back,
walking through days that seem alike, the false contentment
gone, the peace of early morning
gone, the chance to re-capture the life that left,
gone.

3:24

AM. The third time in three days,
the tenth in two weeks, glowing amber
through the darkness of early morning
radiating from a nightstand clock, fixed exactly
on the date you were born, in a line of sight
from the edge of my bed. 3:24 without an attached year
since years carry only vague pieces of suspended time
and, as years pass, it's the moments that stay in place
moving silently to the next year, over years.
And in each of them, there's no mention
of clouds or clarity or any state of mind.

But for now, the clock's numbers stay crisp
without semblance of what was
and in an instant change, lost and unretrievable,
while my breathing goes on
whether or not I want it to.
But some nights, time passes
without a whisper, a sudden blip
gone before I've noticed, the night evaporating
to awakening daylight, coming 'round
to another moment, a different one that feels familiar,
to yet another that looks different, one of many
immeasurable things among this new ordinary.

If Only

It's those words in the smaller pairings
that offer imagined depth but inexact dimension
with eyes that cannot see newness
in weakened light and absent color,
words that can be read
from the ashes of what never was
in a time escaping into the dimming sunset:
if only I could see my choices replayed,
if only I could hold them
when the air was younger,
when they floated on a gentle breeze
and were touched by an earlier sunlight
when I knew what it was
to be in the moment
and I was captured by words
still to come. If only they were here,
if only the words I heard then
continued to speak now.

Chapters

I stood where I left you,
in the vast emptiness of a hollowed canyon,
the sun having set just an hour before
with the whip of the wind
    in the cold dimming light,
in the clamor of birds
    quivering in the trees,
       and the flat sounds of crickets reeling.
This is when you stood
from that moment alone, separate
on a separate journey, perhaps in despair,
    certainly not following the script
    we practiced and rehearsed together.
The house is little more than a blank space
    of echoing walls, silent floors
    and dry candlelight
in the real rooms and the real stillness,
in the calm eye of real vacancy,
    and in the thick drapery
    hanging before darker windows,
    now the workshop of awkward mementos,
        trinkets that whimper for attention—
        uncharted, detached, abandoned.

The Aroma of Despair

You walked in
through the unlocked door
taking bread from my unlocked pantry
then sat by the warmth of the fire
I helped stoke   dwelling here
for as long as I offer welcome.

Listen: that which created you wasn't made
by your hands—but I sustain you.

I'll soon gather strength
and be done with your arrogance.
Between you and me, I'm the one
who holds the cards.

It's taken time, but I see your plan.
I see your callousness
but you see too, it's more about
what lingers.

Your cruel voice speaks
for only yourself, into the depths of my soul
I hear you, but won't let you
take it as your own.

Appearances

My resoluteness doesn't share grief's sadness
many want no part of.   I surrender differently:
in pain that no longer looks like pain—moving from rescue
to mere recovery.

Surely I've become the one thing I too wanted
no part of: an envy overtakes me—
I see the fullness that still resides in others.

Am I joyless for the sake of living
without joy or is the joylessness
shattered by the fate of acceptance?

Am I to remain an oarless boat wandering a lake
fooling whomever sees me
as I float directionless without aid of a rudder
no one knows is missing?

Another Day

A thin rain has been falling. It soaks the air in each room
in a musty melancholy and frees it
to float and hug the walls and shudder along the ceiling.

It seems a long time since the day began.
The hours pass through one window
       and then on through another
stretching the day's shadows
       to blend with the arriving darkness.
On a corner of the kitchen table, days of delivered mail
lay unopened. A brochure on *River Cruises*
sits at the top, the clear-plastic edge-seals
undisturbed, the contents unexplored.
My memories waft across each room
and make their way back to our days
when what lay ahead gave comfort to each moment.

Oh, how I wish I could roll back time,
alter the how, the when, and grasp the why of your leaving,
but only emptiness returns to sit with me,
only what can never be flourishes in the moistened air
while what I've known struggles through each minute
tangled and thrashing in a fishnet cast into the sea.

Night Falling

Now the changes have stopped and what it's come to
has settled in   a curtain masking as it spreads
so what was at one time discernible is painted
in thicker darkness.   At this point I see it will not reverse
another day weathered   another string of moments
shaded by insistence—soundless sketches of how real objects
appear bloodless   stripped of their depth   blended
with their variances.

It's not the daylight I miss   but the touch
of what once stood before me   the comfort seeing it
knowing it was there in the light   now both unreachable.
It's the darkness that seems to hold the more natural light
among the new air that's turned cold shifting
between two selves: one that knows
what the daylight once gave and the other that knows
when the light returns   each day will be different.

Water Flowing

It takes on a life of its own
within the outline of its jaggedly carved pathway.

Who can say where the river began:
a mysterious place upstream in another time?

But I've seen that water runs from different beginnings
to its own destinations   flowing in but one direction
the way each life moves from then
to the here and now. The force of what has accumulated
pushing to this end, to this time, to this place
where others I'd known are no longer
in my here and now
having moved to their separate destinations
flowing along the waters of their journey—
in the distance lives flow to points of arrival
where I have yet to meet them, while others flow
to points of departure, in the deep darkness
of a moonless night carried by the waterflow
where I will never again meet them.

In Its Own Time

In those sun-drenched days
when you were living,

days which we later learned
seem to have been numbered:

when you whispered of forewarning
as if it spoke to you

through the touch of a finger
tracing your life-line along your palm,

the lingering sunlight widening the forest's shadows
where sunlight and darkness work against each other:

one's presence rising, the other fading
pressing on in their decided directions

in their own time coexisting and overlapping
across the scope of moments

through mornings and over afternoons
for what seems a lifetime ago

never moving exactly
how I thought they would,

never sounding exactly how I thought they could,
perforated at different times

by different birds chattering in different tongues,
the whip of a breeze carrying a foretelling winter chill,

sunlight in its warming splendor most vulnerable—
shadow then darkness now the most constant.

Grief's Whispers

Her promise was withheld
when her whispers tumbled into the canyon
and up over the open fields
where the vineyards lay catching chilled water
falling from a sky of doubt
and how easily she cast uncertainty
deciding wistfully whether to moisten the parched earth
or saturate it when there was already enough,
zigging   zagging   rising   falling
rarely in the right amounts   fading into the false daylight
when her promise was all there was
a hope through its own silence
providing a whisper of what was yet to come
but didn't.
And so a new ending is now spoken
carried among the scent of moistened leaves
and the sounds of words that could have been—
but weren't.

Sunset's Fashion

It's in the rhythm of color   a caress
contours chosen which won't overlap   designed
to bring joy   a sense of earthly-beauty
defined differently through quills over time:
the inconsistencies in each add dimension   shout difference.
Yet something is always intentionally hidden—
just enough to bring inquiry.   Below the surface
swirls of conflict storm meaning there are moments
we run from   about a time that ended
or we move to distractions that take our attention:
we count stars or   despite hope   cut down
the large oak tree that's been dying for years.
And with cloud-zippers and buttons   form sleeves
that wrap the sky in colorful cloth and glitter.
I see a spirit in the sky that catches sunset's light
carries it   wraps it in a twirl or a bow
seen by two different selves: I know what I carry
to each end   each sunset leaving   while you know nothing
of the sort   I know what is revealed by the angled sunlight
but you can only imagine.

Knowing

It was in the late days of autumn, those standalone days
when earth cools and thoughts of summer have long faded,

when I'm struck by how permanent
each of the seasons feels while I'm in them

yet how quickly the passing days, and what was thought
permanent, changes.

How quickly the skin forgets the warmth of the summer sun
and that which was thought durable   is gone.

How quickly uncertainty stirs the branches of the trees
knowing they will bend to reach the brightest light

yet unsure how they will endure
through the colder, more variable weather.

And not only permanence fades
there is absence: birds lost   their voices silenced,

bees and insects, their stuttering buzzing gone.
Gone too are what was known

and what was expected
when what was counted on has changed,

when each new day is cloaked in the deception of knowing
with any durability fleeting,

when we cannot think further than our knowing reaches
while we're in them.

Marionette

I feel the coarse strings
tugging at my arms, lifting bent wings
then setting them down,
awkwardly pulling on each leg
to step along a path
I've not chosen, watching ahead
as it swerves and dips
making my gait stiffer, more arrhythmical,
unable to do anything but see
the imbalance between the parts and the whole.
Since you flew on, anguish presses its limits
in the cruelest choreography.

How did my days and nights
come to be so different,
days that dangle in a chilling wind
swirling and following me
where I struggle in their icy contempt
each one shaping how I stand or how I walk
to slowly lose sight of those lively yesterdays
only wanting them to still be here tomorrow,
those packaged, hopeful times when each of us
believed they were endless, into these vulgar days
of solitude, absurdity
and unwillingness.

As Well

To go along   avoid ripples   acquiesce
and surrender to the forces you believe loom larger
but after a time realize   joining is not always agreeing
where once you went along to avoid it
in a kind of abdication.   The challenge was in hearing
its harsh voice   believing loss would somehow resolve
and you would accept what's come to pass
give in   go along
the way it can take a while to see despair
as a lullaby at a slower speed—a more subtle deception
to be recognized   as if avoidance will coat deeper sorrow
and   in a more reassuring light   lead you
to a smoother body of water:
the ripples surrender in place   acquiescence achieved
at the price of leading the hopeful
by the bitter taste of longing no one can discern.

Regret

why didn't I say it,
complete the sentence, finish the thought,
    not in hateful words that couldn't be
    reclaimed, but in loving words
waiting unsaid,
those that may have changed an ending,
those that could have reset time,
those still weathering
    on the tip of my tongue

Miserable Comfort

I know it's not their fault, yet can't help thinking
these are some of my longest known friends
offering few or no words in the rock-strewn valleys
of those moments   and still now, who were, on past days,
the essence of caress in the carefree laughter
centered on living, those who have since disappeared
into a dark forest speaking innocent words
unknowingly inflicting pain or never speaking
any words
for fear they will do the same
and so say nothing
about what goes missing.

I guess it was too much for them to stay with it
for as long as was needed—is still needed—
enduring with me what alone am barely able to carry
into each hour and
into the day of my last breath
as though any small sign of my revival
says the heartache is "over"
and what had been before
can now resume,
in the silence of what stays unspoken
even while other words rush to the surface
about what is now and what is planned for another time—
as though it matters.

The Cloak

It rests squarely on my shoulders shrouding acceptance
and a heart that once beat distinctly
melting the chilled, early-morning moisture
and among whispers of a new day
filled with more than just daylight,
when birds saw what they at once had recognized
and trees and flowers knew what they were witnessing
but now holds shallow breaths in these new mornings.
The honey, the grainy sugar, the dense sweetness
lost to the bitter edges of these newest days,
their heavy yet transparent yoke not set aside
to hang on a hook or stuffed in a closet   this dark
yet transparent cloak I carry
across my shoulders no one knows is there   —
                            but me.

Broken Branches

It's the broken tree branches   fallen
and their suffering   I recognize

the swaying branches that remain
offer their tears   but are helpless to restore

what has tumbled. I feel
their desperate pleas resisting   surrendering

in the same moment   I can sense their grief
share their vulnerability

stuck and unable to alter what has been torn
from what goes on living.

And it's the stark sunlight that renders
the branches' motion more visible

its dabbed white paint on their leaves bobbing
the stirred consequence of what moves them

beyond their wishes   beyond their understanding
beyond their silent prayers.

Breaths

They are for what still knows

what it means when another is without them

their soul needs none of them

so, it alone, in the two worlds

we know and imagine

cannot be anywhere

while being everywhere—

a struggle

between presence and permanence.

Soulful

Can a soul carry regrets
and does it then hold them for eternity?
Can it change what came
      when bound to a body
and not gain wisdom or see a better path
      when it couldn't before?
Can it traverse that body unfixed and floating
or does it hold what it has known
      somehow within it
becoming a part of its sense and its whispers?
Or to a soul are such matters irrelevant
      captured only in earthliness and gravity?
      Are they freed by the unphysical
      in the unseeing and sightlessness
infused with everything there is to know
      without a tongue to speak its wisdom
      to anyone? Does a soul carry on
      from where it left off
waiting for the rest they've known
      to catch up and is time unknown
      and unmeasured, does it wait
      circling the sky and clouds among the air
      and in the trees and along earth's contours
to start again based on its wants and wishes
      or its surrender?

Circuition

Here I go again, passing through my sixth decade,
but this time on a bus
and in other decades pacing or running through each
hoping someone would have, just once,
called out to stop me or take me by a hand
and slow me down.

But this time, the ride is painfully slow,
the lift and fall of each roadway imperfection
coming up through the seat of my pants
and there beside me,

                behind me,
                            before me
the stiff and empty seats, shadowed, worn
each carrying my expectations
like a bag of empty groceries, their faces
paled in the hazy sunlight angling
through the windows, tangling the recollections of those
who once sat there   mingled with the musty air
and the smoke of spent diesel fuel.

Callings

A grieving father calls out for his lost son

the clear sky is just temporary,
    it has no ears, no tongue,
    imagines heaven
    while whistling

gathering clouds come to blanket the sky
    and call to the darkening daylight,
        the heavy rain held within them
    calls out when it's released,
        stays silent when it's ended

in night's darkness, the awakened stars
    call from each birthplace
    trembling in the vast blackness,
their watery eyes go on weeping,
    still chasing their light into emptiness

what stays in darkness no wisdom comes to,
    and there's no consent decreed—
        it languishes in the sunlight
            erased of meaning.

Unrequited

It is the sound I long for:
the melody of a meandering stream
wrapping its arms around what wades into it,
the touch of the warmer water
faded. I search for the sounds
of common language, the deep
eyes, the broad smile
I believe I let go, but the air I inhale
still labors in helplessness.
In the many questions swirling in a maze of words
lost, the grammar across our worlds
absent, a string of longing, the pain
of what stays empty.
I imagine locking a door to keep what was placed inside
alive, but what had been there still escapes
unclaimed. Into the depths of what stays missing:
my shallow breath, my unreturned answers,
I stretch my hand seeking to nurture
a butterfly that stops on a leaf fluttering,
unaware my hand is reaching, waiting.

Phases

On the fourth day after
the anniversary of your leaving
I look back and see I've gone through phases
not just one pass through each
as though once will reset terms to settle
on some firmer ground   but over and over I return
to each one in random order.
Shock and anger then disbelief, which remain,
and back again to anger which peaks in intense debate
about what went wrong
and the helplessness then swarming,
about a benevolent God that forgot me
when I then come to thoughts of acceptance and hope
and think I've made it clear when suddenly
the anger returns and I bargain
for another chance to redraft history.

These cycles   these unwanted strangers gathering
remaining long after I've asked they leave,
long after I sat haunted by their dreadful stares,
their evil eyes, their cold and silent heartlessness,
even while each didn't utter a word
or ever raise a hand.

Pinky Swear
For my son Rick, 1985-2022

Promise me you'll be alright
now that night has come
and the chill in the air
brings loss to my bones. Promise me
you won't run yourself ragged
as you were accustomed doing,
focusing on every little thing and that you know
what it means to have been loved
and to have vaulted past life's challenges, except the one
that took you entirely by surprise. Promise me
you'll remember. Promise me you'll be comforted
in this longest sleep leaving from your time
and in those moments that were later than we could know,
without a sketched plan, spoken or written. Promise me
you'll return at the oddest times and in the strangest places,
in the guise of an occasional hummingbird darting
or through the windings of my sleep
when I've yet to awaken or in the new daylight hour
bright with clarity, in all I've come to and still believe
what I cannot see, pointing your soul in my direction
like a compass that guides to what is settled,
while I watch the earth remain paused
even while it's still turning.

The Aroma of Disappointment

It is not regret but an absence I know
on a walk alone down the sloping grade
becoming more jagged as I stay on it
and tears more harshly at my step
where past it I can see ahead
a hollowed cave in firm rock
under the gray peak of a mountain.
It echoes nothing, it offers no color,
doesn't speak to why it formed
or how it may have been hollowed,
everything is there   but the story.
In the swirling winds around it
and those that rush into it,
nothing is said of those who lived there
or the language they may have spoken,
all the words are missing in the sentences
that do not return, in the words no one heard,
so no one answers, silent grief
over what had been known—
just a dark, hollow cave
left wide open.

Grief

This is what thickens the blood,
        this anger, this sorrow
        this pain and its injustice.
The loss of what is lost,
        this tragedy, this absence,
        this despair.
And how can life resume when it is frozen
        without purpose,
        without meaning?
How will tranquility come
        and how will I know its peace,
        its comfort, its serenity?
I try to move on
        initiating distractions,
        but a knife-edge of guilt
        cuts at the thought of leaving
        what's lost behind.
I've been cheated, but what's been lost
        has been cheated more,
            wishing time could be stopped
            and moved backwards.
Wishing it were different.
        Wishing it never happened.

Days of Summer

Those oaky days have ended, those filled
with the nose of breathtaking complexity
stir no longer, swept away like the skins
of spent grapes and the finish dwindling on the tongue.

How could we know this was to be
the last sandy-haired, dried-skin summer, raw and rich
when soothing nighttime breezes from an ocean nearby
would be stilled and murmurs of its motion
were to grow more distant, when seagulls,
who had run along the sand, scavenged all there was
and when there remain only questions
about why days must change? Is it always a benevolent
God's Will that what is given should then be
taken? Is this the way change is to be imposed:
ripe glimpses of extraordinary aromas replaced
by the isolation of inodorous ones, sundrenched-warmth
replaced by swirling winds and biting chill?
Are we always to be left with different species of birds
gathering as they begin to leave, awaiting some signal
to tell them time has come? Or is it to be made
solely of acceptance of a time ended, a different one begun,
of full-bodied foliage and their absorbed hues
fading in the paling sunlight, the dulled luster of what we had
and can be no longer?

Balance

When my sense of the ebb and flow is lost
and everything I hear and everything I speak
    carries only the mood of loss,
    when everything is witness
    to wickedness, even the warmth
    of early-morning sunlight
    or the refreshing rain at night,
when I know the bloomed dogwood's leaves
are still reaching in the gentlest soothing breeze,
    but all I hear are its delicate flowers
    shouting in a waterfall of litter,
    and when I sense the shadows broadening
    but only see daylight leaving
and can recognize the familiar ground
but can only see it covered in weeds,
    then my sense of this mourning time,
    in the scorched moonlight burned black,
    will never run its course,
    after times when everything was enough
    but the peaks in each of them
    have vanished.
I didn't ask for this, but I do ask now
to rescue my sense of the ebb and flow
    in everything I hear and in everything I see
to continue on and restore my sense of balance.

SECTION TWO

Dispersion

It was there in moments thick as daylight
    in forms with which I was familiar:
in the beauty and depth of those moments
    and cherished for the shortest time,
    under the shade of old trees
    and their dense bark,
    under older clouds that I learned
    can gather over everything that breathes,
and beside the old water of a pond
    that despite its time,
        still glistens like diamonds.
It stood in the wake of what each passed through,
swaying under the long branches in sunlight,
    in the brief air, the vanishing color,
    there before us in the hours of the oceans
    and in the songs of the mourning doves and sparrows
    who sing under the morning's waning moon.
Now I have only their sounds and images,
only the time I spent and had taken
and, in its varied colors, only the old days
holding their breaths, waiting.

Birth Dance

The potency comes to remain—
for a time,
permeating the deep grass reaching
skyward, unabated, inhaling air,
sipping cool crystal water, flooded
by a need to sustain life's breath
as it surges effortlessly,
when all of life's promises hang in the balance
as if the path taken holds choices
like dog-eared pages offer words
only certain eyes recognize.
But what if there are days that drain the dance,
stricken the eyes, deepen the dark patches under them,
those set on a course that come
despite wailing or cooing, despite promise
and the sustenance of what's to be and cannot match
its beauty again, to then leave what was abandoned
adrift in breezes that turn colder
when the wind suddenly changes course,
the way the depth of fallen snow blown by it
can only be known in new daylight,
the way impulse is not permanence and what thrives
comes to be impervious to what surrounds it,
the way the birth dance ages, flattens out,
moves on.

Postmortem

It's been said after the death of a child
of any age, you emerge much stronger.
I know nothing of strength or emergence
only know of what sits in my sight no longer.
The sun does not paint the trees
in the same bright yellows of early morning,
the sky's grays and blues
are stretched and faded.

I think what they mean to say
is the eyes come to see differently,
come to wisdom in beams of light
that slices what's unimportant
to pieces.
Yet I know less of peace and its tranquility—
nothing of wanting strength
or how what emerges
would itself be wanted.

But then, some things worth having
are not living: the sea's thick air and the spray
of salt-water thrown from its crashing waves,
the sight of clouds sailing across the horizon,

the sky, the moon, the stars,
none of them living
but still in their own way breathing,
still worth living to behold.

New Light

When dawn comes   new light brightens in steps
without a switch to flood morning in daylight
speaking gradually in one-word sentences
building upon each one. New light speaks to
what darkness had muffled
telling of potential and its patience.
This is its will   its dogged drive   its prayer
even when the darkest days say so much
about what can stay wrong. It comes despite clouds
that say "no" windlessly without emotion.
It comes despite darknesses' intention
with reassuring hands on each shoulder
to repeat words that free you   echo clarity
dampen despair. The new light knows how to fill blackness
mute shadows   take you by the hand
intwined like roots to permeate your blood
and course a subtle river the rain fell into
and was then carried away by.
The new light keeps in its care what we asked for
even if it is only to reassure   offer choices.
New light knows nothing of time   sees nothing
except in subtle hues that tint what it's fallen upon
leaving its imprint even after it has gone.

Sunlight in Fall

You are hidden openly
on the trees' quivering leaves,
    on their darkened branches and outstretched arms,
    and through the crisp air of the moment.
I saw you not long ago
    on brighter days
    speaking to the promises you made
        now no longer,
    a flame that doesn't know
        from where it came
        and soon forgets its light.
And by late afternoon on these gray days
        you are stale, weaker, yet oddly richer
        in the colors you ignite,
        loved heartbreakingly
        through your waning,
among the birds that clamor
        and will soon be gone,
through the trees shedding their changing leaves,
and among the wildflowers that fade
    despite one's wishes—
when all at once, the gemstone-stars
    fill the whole sky in the dark night,

    through watery eyes
    and escaping streaks of clear light
        offer fresh hopes and reasons
        even in their redundancies,
    with no end in sight.

Vibes

Soon after you left,
    in the darkness of night's drowsiness,
I hear footsteps
    walk across the bedroom floor
and later in the day, see a hummingbird call
    hovering above the hanging impatiens,
and watch the monarch butterfly
    wearing a yellow and black sweater
    flutter close to my chest
                  then float away,
and I hear those words you often said
    without a sound, telling me again
    you'll walk beside me in the darkness
    and in the brighter light of day.

Feel the Noise

I've come to this silent place
to hear what I've not heard,
beneath the rubble of what has fallen

where I am unable to move
and unable to free myself,
in a time hearing no sound
holding no texture, holding no density.

The sounds of prior times live in this small space
holding little oxygen, in the shallow breaths
that barely keep the sounds alive.

I know no peace while aching
to feel the noise again, to see daylight
run its hands over me
and feel the oxygen surge,
hear what hasn't been heard
and feel the sounds of uproar,
telling me there are many voices still to hear
many voices talking from what they alone know,
what they alone feel
if they could talk all at once.

Solstice Shadows

It's the subtlety of shadows
that tells us we're in motion,

and we come to confirm it
when looking out past the window

when the angle of the sun
changes the shadow the poplar casts.

It's the subtlety of shadows that tells us
where we've been and where we're headed

as if a fortune teller who can foresee
the future in the sun's complexion

and gives consent as the sun goes away
to change the colors it reflects from the trees' raucous leaves

which have never known their real color being
unable to stay painted the way they first were.

And we see it in the stars, moon, and clouds
who glide through the thinned trees

in the glow of a nighttime sky,
even though the sun travels at midnight

to carry its slowly-changing shadows across the air.
Our time changes along with them,

when our shadows come to cast a longer, more despairing
shadow each unfolding in their own time

and watching the stars for a glimpse of what is to come,
what will remain, and what will return under the oddness

of an expanding sun at the height of the dead
of winter, in cycles farther and nearer than we can recognize.

Early Morning Light

Before there is light there are smiles
filled with intent
        aspiring thoughts
sober thoughts
        of just what this day could be
then brightening light
          radiating
        to the trees and flowers
        to bumble bees and butterflies
        at work and smiling too
just us alone in this new morning light
under the common deepening-blue heavens
my older   self knowing what it sees now
not wanting to know anything
of what my younger self could not see
        when intent to find what it was I'd imagined
then with so few thoughts of that younger time
in this older time
carried by the same light of that earlier time
but with each early morning
gone
so that what I'd seen in those earlier times
left without leaving a gift.

I don't recall many smiles then
I don't recall the early morning light
        or if there were bees or flowers
though I am sure they were there
in that forgotten time
        in the early morning light
when I was distracted and simply missed them.

Occhi e Orecchie

Another day gives hope to what's wished
yet there are some things, despite pleading,
    that will never change.
But my heart still beats resolutely
even when my eyes and ears know
    this hollowed space will remain forever,
when what had been
moves to the here and now—
just as a summer rain arrives.
It rattles the empty gutters where I listen
for the droplets, learning from them:
click……..click…click…click……click
and, if I am open to their random code
tapping in a foreign language, and take them in,
I can see they offer their purposeful water
one drop at a time, each speeding to earth
to find their own leaf at a common speed, landing
in their own place, and each time they come,
the pattern changes. The droplets' deliberateness swells
to embrace me, and if I listen intently,
I can hear its tempo smooth to a heartbeat
that mirrors mine, becoming more
routine, more familiar.

And moments later   the rain moves on.
And moments later, I see good in the simplest things,
    and my eyes and ears are open
    to what they take in,
as I come to understand this foreign language
    and know its promise
    carried across each moment.

Voices After Tragedy

In plumes of newest song   I hear
what anyone else can too: this message
about how time can stand still
against a gray-streaked sky and other weather
and shield no boundary   a continuous circle
with deep shadows   and despite time passing
never forgotten   this shallow wind
tipping the thickest oaks   moving
without the help of a compass—all the years heard at once
all the notions of what comes and leaves
within these plumes of song   these new embracing voices
heard after every storm.

A Pact With Nature

In early spring, the mild-yellow pollen-winds
swirl across the open meadow
and ally with the fiery robin red-breast
to conspire to end thawing winter's frozen prison.
I walk the newly-liberated field
and see a leaf tumbling in the chilled March wind,
rolling atop the cool cropped-grass
no longer breathing, an arthritic page of gray hope—
remains of a deeply-bleached photograph.
I watch its uneven progress across the field,
yet just a few months before, it sat a majestic prince
dressed in emeralds and diamonds
perched atop a balcony speaking boldly
to its loyal subjects, now dethroned and unfamiliar
aimlessly wandering a harsh, annihilated land.

How can something so radiant be lost?
How is something so essential discarded
so bitterly—much worse than being an orphan
aimlessly seeking whatever peace may be found,
to come to rest and still remain captive
even while the life it had known had been taken.

But for now in the chill of daylight, the open field
grows softer in every direction:
the earth has moved on to this renewed place
where the sun blankets it more completely
and I can see and hear the busyness of early bees
floating across the meadow and birds laughing
through the branches of the reawakening trees. And I think
this is the time when they renew their pacts with sunlight.

And while I don't yet feel it, I realize this too
is my time to reach another pact with nature,
inhaling the aromas of what I cannot see,
warily enjoying the motion and sounds of what I can
take in, watching the streaming water as it returns
with vigor, revitalized by this continuous pact
I am part of. And in this new time, I still see you
as you were, remaining with me through every day
as I struggle with what's been lost then remade
only to then have it lost again, this ridiculous cycle
I haven't the wherewithal to alter.

No Rest with Just Silence

There is no rest in silence.
There is no peace in silent rest,
for silence alone is not enough,
it alone does not permit
silent calm, the storm still swirls
in silent fury,
a silent blizzard,
a snow globe of commotion:
silent, unheard.

I have seen the lack of silent peaceful rest.
I have seen the silent snow fall
onto a silent forest floor. I have seen
the silent snowfall bring peace,
its snowfall melody bringing silence to the commotion,
its snowfall melody bringing peaceful silent rest
if its melody be heard, if its silent peaceful melody
be heard, the silent snowfall melody
a distraction to the silence.

The Moment At Evening

It comes over many moments gathered
like harsh grains of salt scattered on a counter   scooped up
with one hand pushing to the other   in faint light
under a solemn piano: the same few notes playing
over and over   the way birds carry music
into a broad sky   each note a sound of their fears   a hand
shadowed by the colors of leaving   each note
a part of evening recited in the parts of grieving   late
and then all at once   a time when I lie awake
listening for the moment at evening when night
can fly on   where I still keep a sign of daylight
waiting 'til morning.

Hills

Toward the hills outside the city limits,
there's a pathway made of irregularly-sized rock
a calling cracked
by the boots of journeymen in a time of their
wanting, in a time of their need.

Then after it, a carved path each alone made
without rumbling machinery or explosives
just worn boots perhaps some walking sticks
made of sturdy cast-away tree branches
to pierce the earth and soften it for their journey.
I've been told the sounds of their footsteps
trudged endlessly through the upwardly-sloping grade,
in amber sunlight and in shadows cast at days end
day-upon-day, step-upon-step for as long as steps
could be taken   hearing no other voice
above their deepened breathing than their own
out onto that path each helped build.

And I see how I can take these paths for granted
and cherish the insight of their creation:
a different effort, but an effort just the same,
to ascend these steeply rising hills
casting aside what must be cast aside,
those moments lived sore and reeling,
to return again to the moments that reach
for the new.

Sight for Sore Eyes

It's been raining for days,
the tree branches drooping
by the weight of water
with the sunshine stuck behind the heavy water
continuing to fall steadily.
And I can see the fattening streams and the roaring water,
the heavier coating spreading across everything
weighing on all that sits on the ground
welcoming the newest water.
And see how balance now returns and sustains
what must thrive: the pain of drought, the dry earth,
the chapped wheat, forgotten,
now flourishing as if the earth became a breast
filling with milk. We thrive, we remember
then we forget
see only what is before us, see only the good,
then the bad, then the good
wrapped in bandages—
yet they come to heal what is broken,
help each reversal with little else to be done
except the waiting.

River in Autumn

The river flows across the gap between two lands
I watch its water rippling in the remaining sunlight,
with one land behind me
    covered by autumn's late-afternoon shadows
and the other ahead
    moving through autumn's amber sunlight,
these two lands stay separated
    for as long as the river itself runs on.
It holds the sort of water
    that can flow for miles
    and not lose its broader shape or speed
yet bend and swell with just the slightest resistance
and fill a path around what stands before it
    so its world is disposed to
        what might change it
    in the times coming
    and in those leaving
    in the miles taken
        and in the miles before it empties
all while emitting a steady whisper
    like the unconsciousness of consciousness
    without regard for time.

Recollections of Water

There's no telling how a mind will recall
what it has known when each passing day
can be threatened within a breath

Retrieved when each is dressed in the clothing
of yesterday. Recollection hugs the walls
and the top and bottom of what it is carried in
like water carried in a ceramic jug,
where the extent of its good is limited
only by its boundaries.

This is what the mind knows, this is the real water
with the contents blending seamlessly,
sipped a bit at a time   drawn from a larger body:
a reservoir of vitality with each drop,
a gift adhering to what it touches—
wellbeing flowing from its openings.

.

Contentment Quotient

the whole time it was a simple equation
arriving in the spring's gentler winds
after the foliage and the wildlife had returned
in the sounds of their eyes
gleaming in the sun's yellow rays,
in the glows of moonbeams and the whiter light
of stars that shudder in the night.

And after looking there, I see
these not so complex formulas are without
the need for any complex thought,
and I see you again my contentment quotient
sitting at the bench where I left you
waiting with the laughter of children playing behind you,
its one use repeated even in all the time that passed
believing I would somehow find you again
in that one place
I just hadn't thought to look   until now

Beyond Question

Inasmuch as our sun is a star
    to dozens of distant planets
    floating beyond our reaches
    each circling their own light
    far away   and we can only see it
    beaming to us
        at night,
and inasmuch as our planet is home
    to billions   we   for all we know
    are not alone surely
        at least one must be home
    to those who fly or walk or need only close
    their eyes and imagine.

And inasmuch as we may think we're alone
we surely cannot be the only place
    where bodies and souls
        speak or breathe and without seeing
            believe.   Some may be far ahead
            in understanding their world's genius
        while others struggle through a time
            we've long surpassed
gripped by a past still evolving but sharing our likeness,

recalling the single place
    we've set out for   like rain
      that knows from where it's come
        and to where it's going
    yet always ends
      in silence.

The silent light from each star
    still beams
    even when its glow may have ended
    knowing it was never ours—
      could never be ours,
        alone.

Amber Sunrise

Brightness appears early this new morning
but I am not ready
to bring this one to daylight
yet can hear its calling
choosing at this moment not to witness it
just wanting to set it on the table like a book
and recount the prior mornings in their splendor
in the dimmed new light coating those early mornings
with its familiar patina, a quiet peace
dispersed by the finer pale-amber mist
reaching for and just touching
what it appears to touch.   But I am here
and in no hurry   imagining
how there can't be a better morning
while I hear the birds
beginning their early routines
singing their unconditional acceptance
of this wonderful yet imperfect place—
a place I've come to and will leave as it is—
        imperfect   unhurried
the way light focuses on what is moving
on what comes to be visible or stays invisible
on what comes into view or leaves it.

Rain Whispers

I've been watching its pattern arrive in the early morning
    in a fabric whose texture is different
    in a thin fog obscuring my view   watching it
    as it blurs what's behind and intertwined with it
a memory of darkness lessening without a photograph
since darkness cannot be photographed.
The arriving rain changes the patterned fabric
    this latest cloth dispersed by the rush of rainwater
    streaming in rivers of mercury
its latest effort to cleanse what was in need of cleansing
and restore what needed restoring
so as it passes can reset all the stars in the sky
and where my dreams go
    and what remained of the night.

And when I look again   the rain too is gone
    silently   unassumingly
followed by a gentle breeze   a whisper
leaving the greens   yellows   reds   to stand dripping—
    glistening gemstones in the returning sunlight.

And I wonder if that's the way it always was: the rains
nudged by the wind   carrying away what must be taken
    moving past the window where I capture its leaving

    in the expanding morning sunlight
watching the whisper of what it takes with it
    but what must have always been taken this way.

In a world where all living things end   little has changed.

The Aroma of Hope

Consider it often arises
from something ending
with glimmers of light still flying,
among the dots and dashes of a foreign
mortal code when what had been lies
motionless on a meadow floor waiting
for life to return and recapture the air
to see the way forward.

Is this the human condition
in dreams and aspirations?
Or the sights and sounds of tragedy?
The hooded executioner
revealed to the masses held off
as long as nameless machines
can hum and play God   and offer hope
things can only get better.
In the heavy air and on the cold, hard floors
and in the light, the bright light
slammed shut
under the lid of Pandora's mythical box
still beaming.

The Aroma of Lilac

Even when life has been confiscated
even when it has been pulled from the earth
where it sat joyfully anchored   assured   confident
after it had graced each gentle breeze
with its robust aroma
and its root-stretched legs
flourished in the sunlight's energy
and it knew both comfort and nurture,
but was then yanked from where it nestled—
could it still find a way to take root again
and thrive?   Burst forth in fragrant breaths
with an endless appetite to go on?
Can it ever resume caring for itself and exhaling
into each moment   endlessly trying to restore
what was so abruptly ended?

And its urges go on   steadily finding new places
where roots can again take hold in the smallest crevices
and reset what was thought lost
where wishes and daylight again push forward
connecting what's crushingly lost with what's still living—
yet never in exactly the same places.

About the Author

SR Inciardi was born in New York City and grew up in Brooklyn, New York attending Brooklyn College of the City University of New York and then New York University. He has been writing poetry since his teen years. SR Inciardi is married and has one married adult child and four grandchildren.

This is SR Inciardi's third collection of poetry. The first, **Coloring Outside the Edges***, was released in October 2022 and the second,* **The Aroma of Thawing***,* **Poems on Grief and Recovery** *was released in June 2023. Both have been made available on Amazon, Barnes & Noble, and other outlets in hardcover, paperback, and eBook versions.*

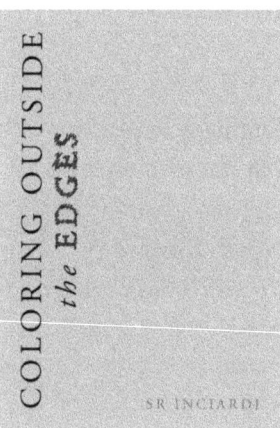 

Acknowledgments

Many thanks to the following magazines and their Editors:

Soulful & ***Broken Branches*** both previously appeared in Front Porch Review

Appearances was published by Grey Sparrow Journal

Birth Dance & ***New Light*** previously appeared in Spillwords

Marionette previously appeared in *Figments*

Early Morning Light & ***The Moment at Evening*** both previously appeared in Written Tales

Postscript

To all those who suffer each day
grieving the loss of a loved one that can never be
replaced, may this book,
written after suffering my own tragic loss,
 provide some measure of comfort,
and may its purpose,
whispered on the pages within it,
provide a pact between us
and in some small measure
offer guidance through these most difficult times:
someone cried,
someone was comforted,
someone was changed for the better.

SR Inciardi

www.ingramcontent.com/pod-product-compliance
Lightning Source LLC
LaVergne TN
LVHW041345080426
835512LV00006B/617